play guitar with...
the blues brothers

AF010549

everybody needs somebody to love
5

gimme some lovin'
12

jailhouse rock
19

theme from rawhide
26

shake a tail feather
34

sweet home chicago
40

guitar tablature explained
2

To access audio visit:
www.halleonard.com/mylibrary

6626-9112-3215-2439

Order No. AM951896

Music compiled an arranged by Arthur Dick

Music processed by Andrew Shiels
Cover photograph courtesy of Ronald Grant Archive
Recordings produced and mastered by Jonas Persson

All guitars by Arthur Dick, Bass by Paul Townsend, Drums by Ian Thomas
Piano & keyboards by Allan Rogers, Harmonica by Stuart Constable
Tenor Sax on 'Sweet Home Chicago' by Alex Ward, Brass arrangements by Allan Rogers
Backing vocals on 'Theme From Rawhide' by The Frith Street Male Voice Choir

ISBN 978-0-71197-123-3

For all works contained herein:
Unauthorized copying, arranging, adapting, recording, internet posting, public performance,
or other distribution of the music in this publication is an infringement of copyright.
Infringers are liable under the law.

Visit Hal Leonard Online at
www.halleonard.com

World headquarters, contact:
Hal Leonard
7777 West Bluemound Road
Milwaukee, WI 53213
Email: info@halleonard.com

In Europe, contact:
Hal Leonard Europe Limited
1 Red Place
London, W1K 6PL
Email: info@halleonardeurope.com

In Australia, contact:
Hal Leonard Australia Pty. Ltd.
4 Lentara Court
Cheltenham, Victoria, 3192 Australia
Email: info@halleonard.com.au

guitar tablature explained

Guitar music can be notated three different ways: on a musical stave, in tablature, and in rhythm slashes

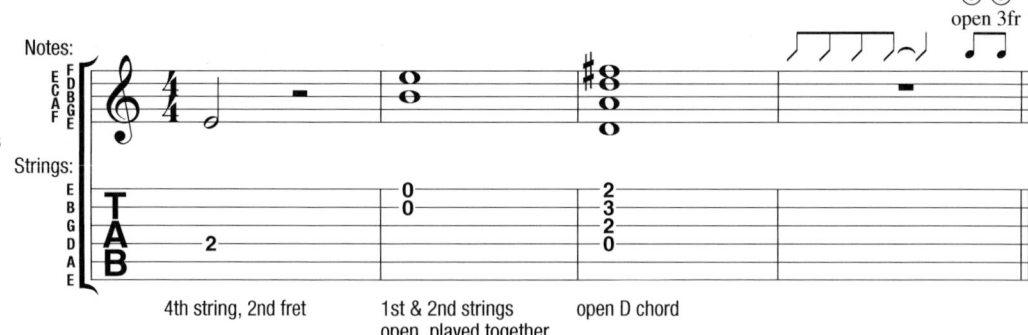

RHYTHM SLASHES are written above the stave. Strum chords in the rhythm indicated. Round noteheads indicate single notes.

THE MUSICAL STAVE shows pitches and rhythms and is divided by lines into bars. Pitches are named after the first seven letters of the alphabet.

TABLATURE graphically represents the guitar fingerboard. Each horizontal line represents a string, and each number represents a fret.

definitions for special guitar notation

SEMI-TONE BEND: Strike the note and bend up a semi-tone (1/2 step).

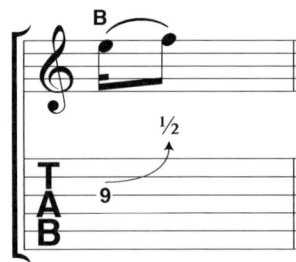

WHOLE-TONE BEND: Strike the note and bend up a whole-tone (whole step).

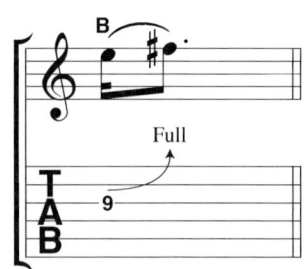

GRACE NOTE BEND: Strike the note and bend as indicated. Play the first note as quickly as possible.

QUARTER-TONE BEND: Strike the note and bend up a 1/4 step.

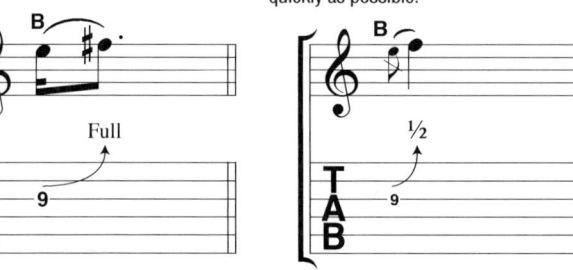
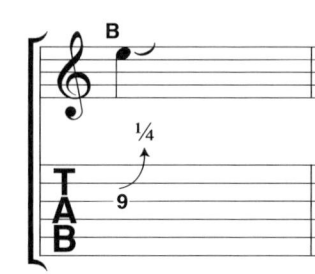

BEND & RELEASE: Strike the note and bend up as indicated, then release back to the original note.

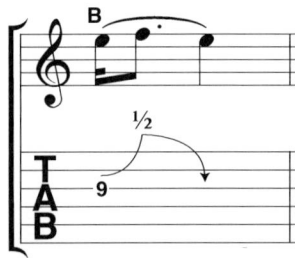

COMPOUND BEND & RELEASE: Strike the note and bend up and down in the rhythm indicated.

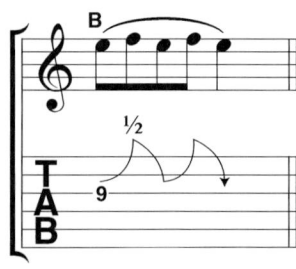

PRE-BEND: Bend the note as indicated, then strike it.

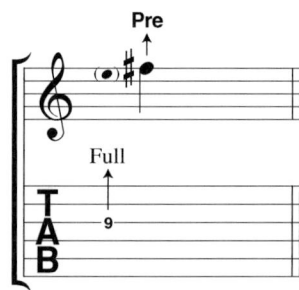

PRE-BEND & RELEASE: Bend the note as indicated. Strike it and release the note back to the original pitch.

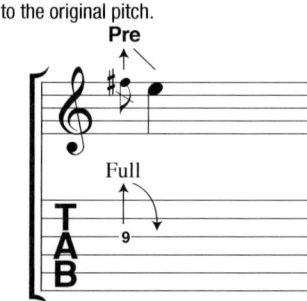

UNISON BEND: Strike the two notes simultaneously and bend the lower note up to the pitch of the higher.

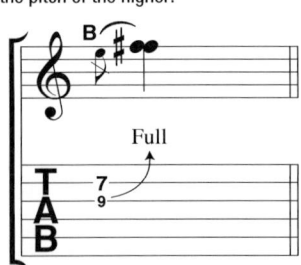

BEND & RESTRIKE: Strike the note and bend as indicated then restrike the string where the symbol occurs.

BEND, HOLD AND RELEASE: Same as bend and release but hold the bend for the duration of the tie.

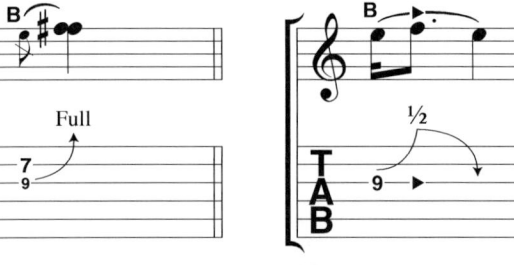
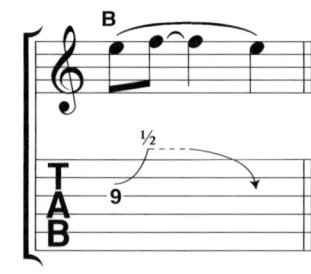

BEND AND TAP: Bend the note as indicated and tap the higher fret while still holding the bend.

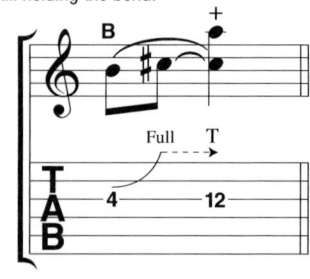

VIBRATO: The string is vibrated by rapidly bending and releasing the note with the fretting hand.

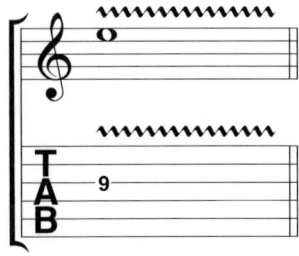

HAMMER-ON: Strike the first (lower) note with one finger, then sound the higher note (on the same string) with another finger by fretting it without picking.

PULL-OFF: Place both fingers on the notes to be sounded, Strike the first note and without picking, pull the finger off to sound the second (lower) note.

LEGATO SLIDE (GLISS): Strike the first note and then slide the same fret-hand finger up or down to the second note. The second note is not struck.

NOTE: The speed of any bend is indicated by the music notation and tempo.

SHIFT SLIDE (GLISS & RESTRIKE): Same as legato slide, except the second note is struck.

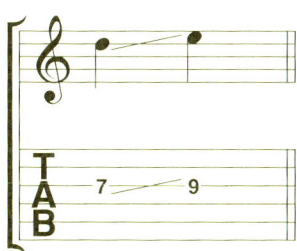

TRILL: Very rapidly alternate between the notes indicated by continuously hammering on and pulling off.

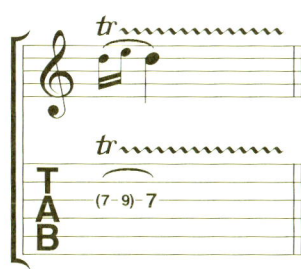

TAPPING: Hammer ("tap") the fret indicated with the pick-hand index or middle finger and pull off to the note fretted by the fret hand.

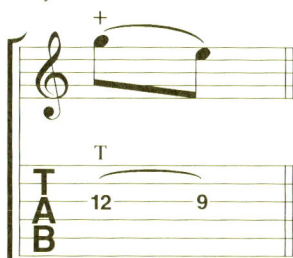

PICK SCRAPE: The edge of the pick is rubbed down (or up) the string, producing a scratchy sound.

MUFFLED STRINGS: A percussive sound is produced by laying the fret hand across the string(s) without depressing, and striking them with the pick hand.

NATURAL HARMONIC: Strike the note while the fret-hand lightly touches the string directly over the fret indicated.

PINCH HARMONIC: The note is fretted normally and a harmonic is produced by adding the edge of the thumb or the tip of the index finger of the pick hand to the normal pick attack.

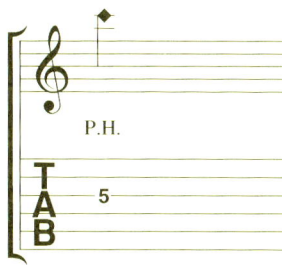

HARP HARMONIC: The note is fretted normally and a harmonic is produced by gently resting the pick hand's index finger directly above the indicated fret (in parentheses) while the pick hand's thumb or pick assists by plucking the appropriate string.

PALM MUTING: The note is partially muted by the pick hand lightly touching the string(s) just before the bridge.

RAKE: Drag the pick across the strings indicated with a single motion.

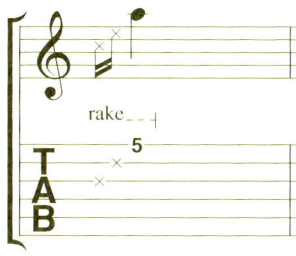

TREMOLO PICKING: The note is picked as rapidly and continuously as possible.

ARPEGGIATE: Play the notes of the chord indicated by quickly rolling them from bottom to top.

SWEEP PICKING: Rhythmic downstroke and/or upstroke motion across the strings.

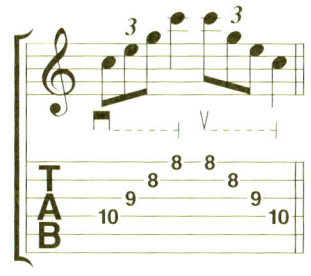

VIBRATO DIVE BAR AND RETURN: The pitch of the note or chord is dropped a specific number of steps (in rhythm) then returned to the original pitch.

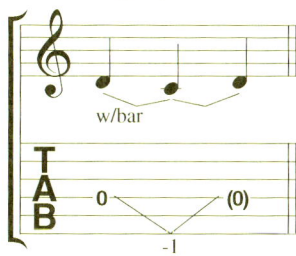

VIBRATO BAR SCOOP: Depress the bar just before striking the note, then quickly release the bar.

VIBRATO BAR DIP: Strike the note and then immediately drop a specific number of steps, then release back to the original pitch.

additional musical definitions

(accent)	•	Accentuate note (play it louder).
(accent)	•	Accentuate note with great intensity.
(staccato)	•	Shorten time value of note.
	•	Downstroke
	•	Upstroke

D.S. al Coda

D.C. al Fine

tacet

- Go back to the sign (%), then play until the bar marked *To Coda* ⊕ then skip to the section marked ⊕ *Coda*.
- Go back to the beginning of the song and play until the bar marked *Fine* (end).
- Instrument is silent (drops out).
- Repeat bars between signs.
- When a repeated section has different endings, play the first ending only the first time and the second ending only the second time.

NOTE: Tablature numbers in parentheses mean: 1. The note is sustained, but a new articulation (such as hammer on or slide) begins.
2. A note may be fretted but not necessarily played.

everybody needs somebody to love

Words & Music by Jerry Wexler, Bert Berns & Solomon Burke

© Copyright 1964 Keetch, Caesar & Dino Music Incorporated, USA.
EMI Music Publishing Limited, 127 Charing Cross Road, London WC2H 0EA (66.67%)/Copyright Control (33.33%).
All Rights Reserved. International Copyright Secured.

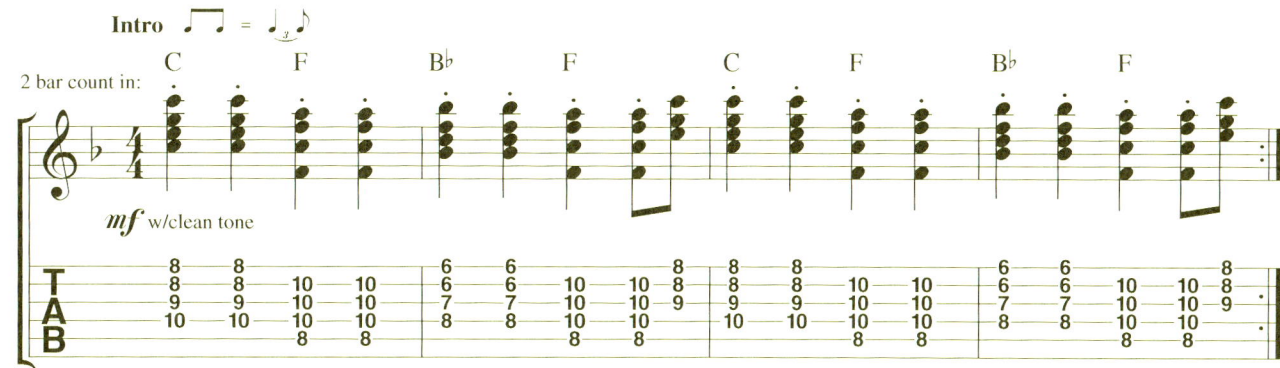

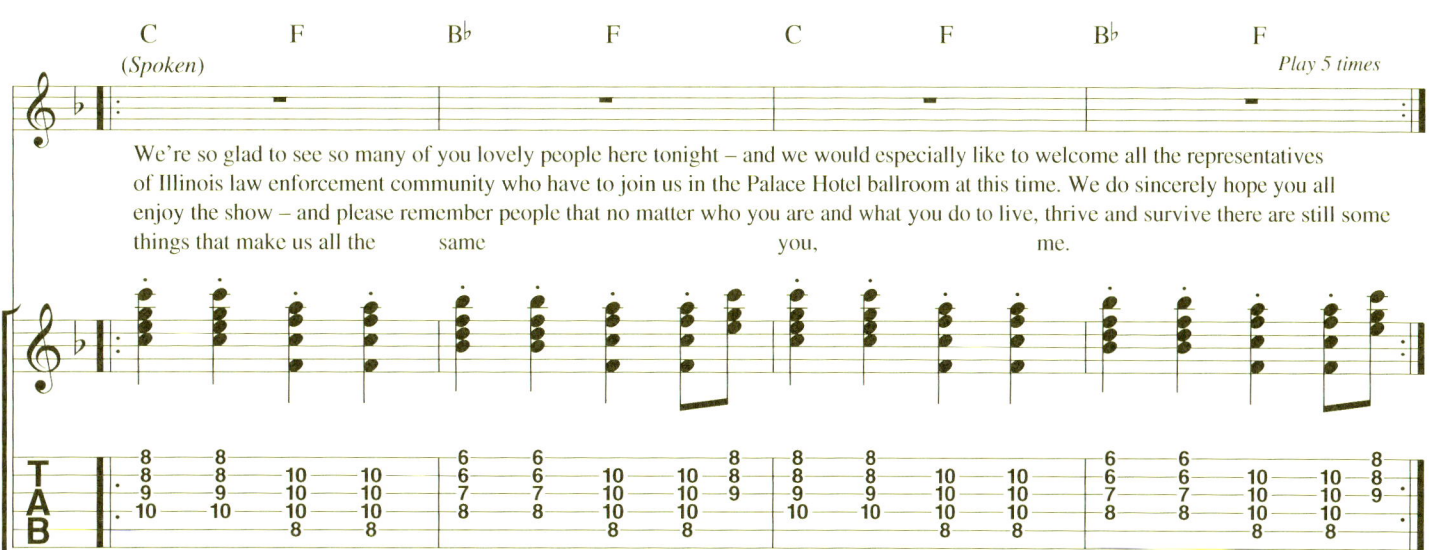

(Spoken) We're so glad to see so many of you lovely people here tonight – and we would especially like to welcome all the representatives of Illinois law enforcement community who have to join us in the Palace Hotel ballroom at this time. We do sincerely hope you all enjoy the show – and please remember people that no matter who you are and what you do to live, thrive and survive there are still some things that make us all the same — you, me.

them, everybody, everybody. Ev-ery-bo-dy

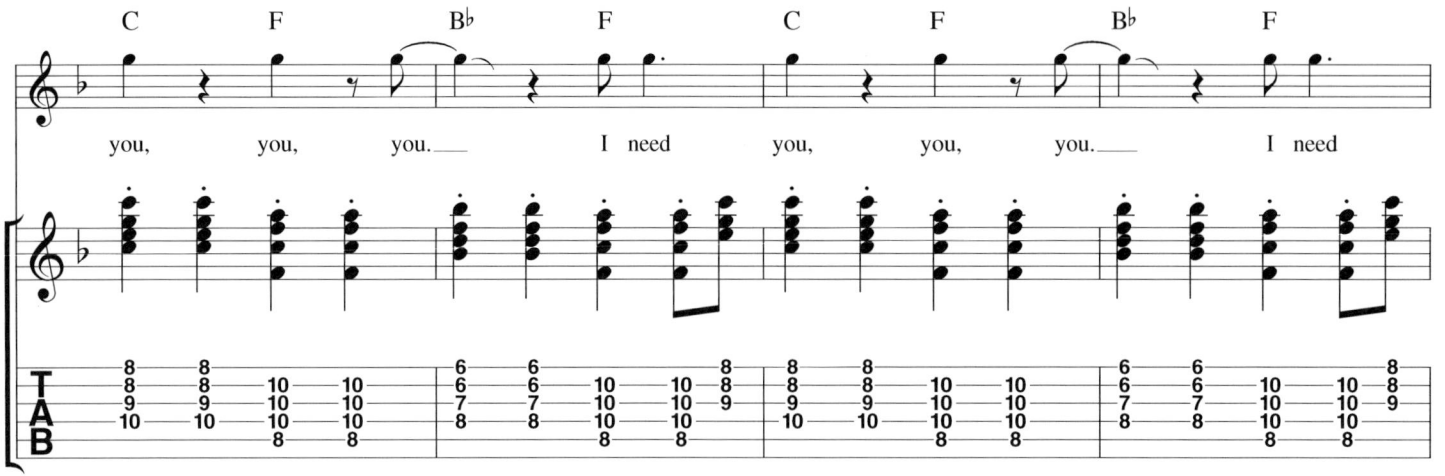
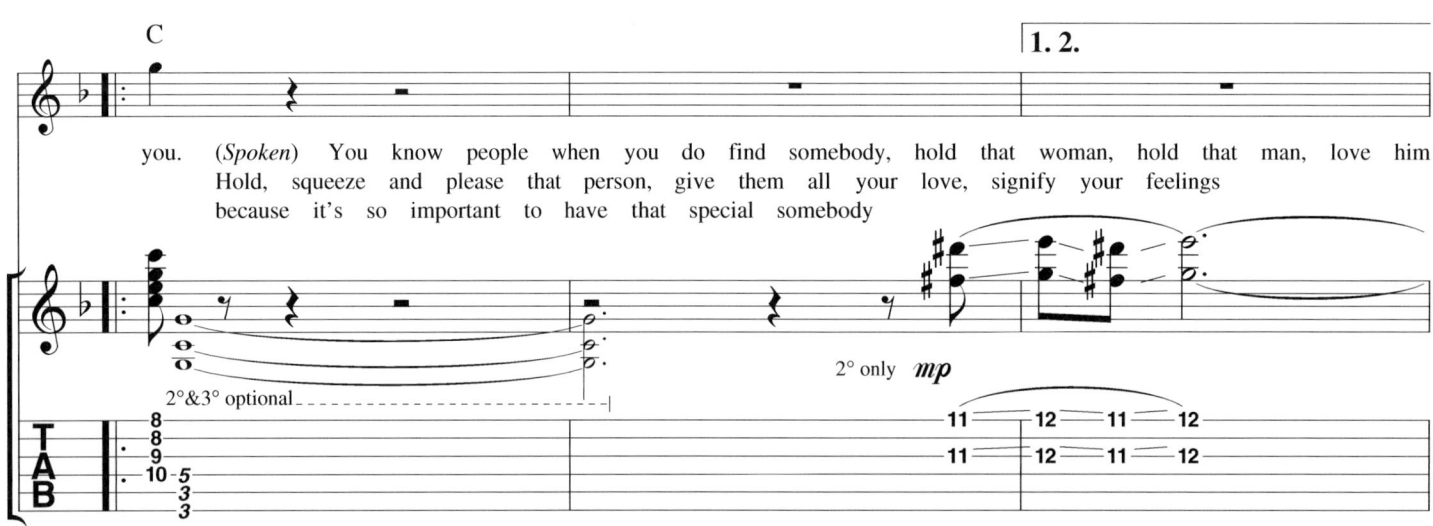
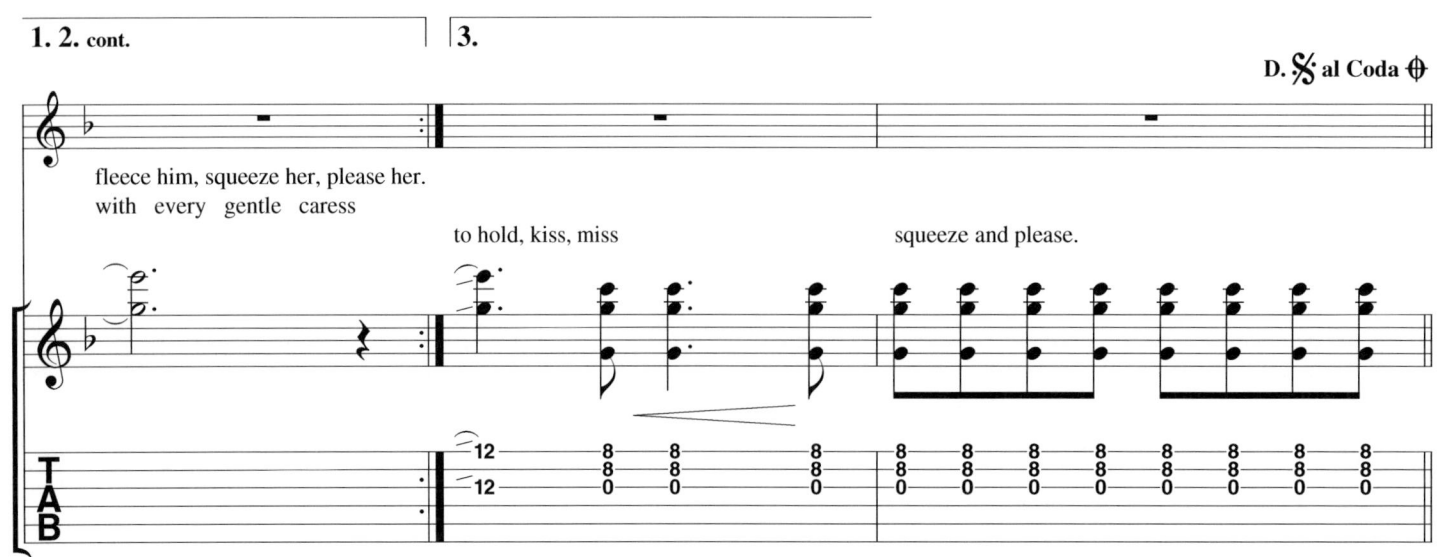

gimme some lovin'

Words & Music by Steve Winwood, Muff Winwood & Spencer Davis

© Copyright 1966 Island Music Limited/F.S. Music Limited.
Universal/Island Music Limited, Elsinore House, 77 Fulham Palace Road, London W6 8JA (66.67%)/
Warner/Chappell Music Limited, Griffin House, 161 Hammersmith Road, London W6 8BS (33.33%).
All Rights Reserved. International Copyright Secured.

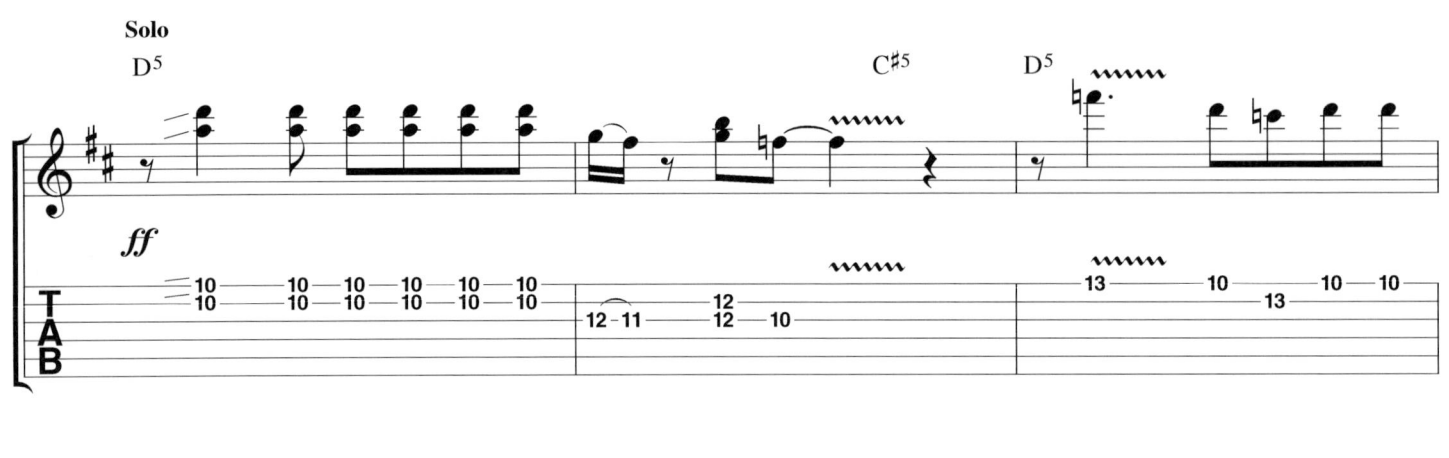
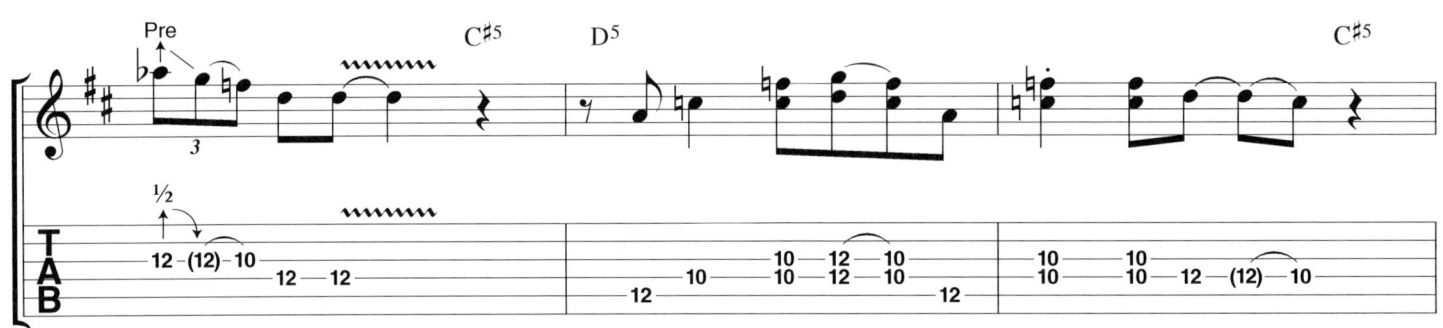
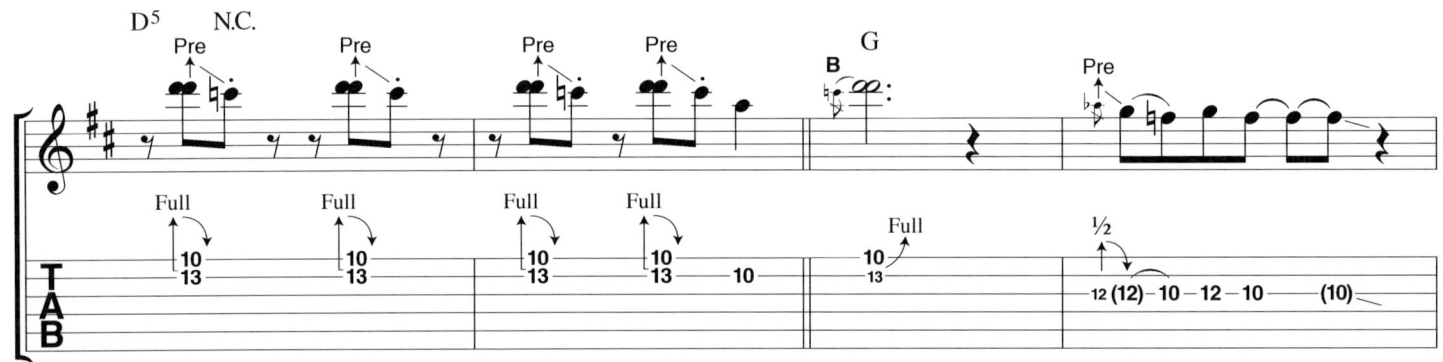
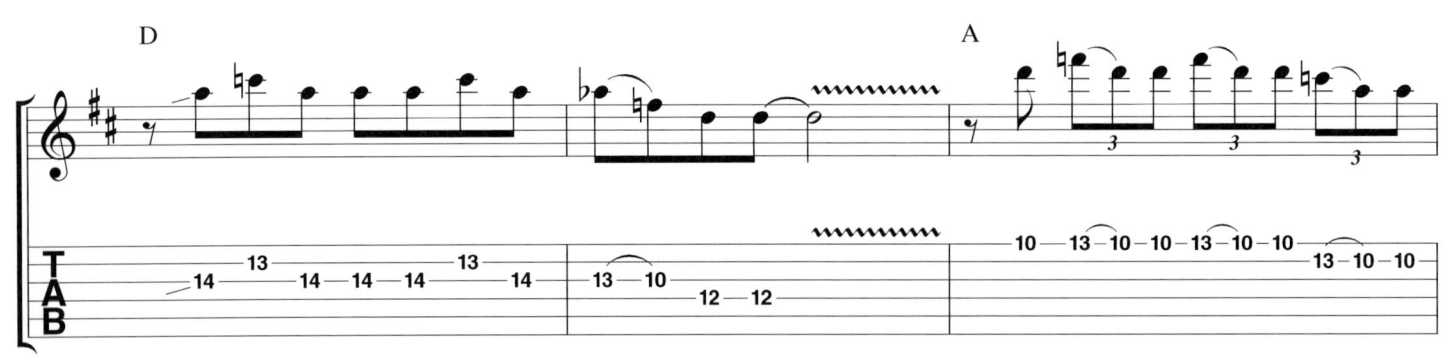
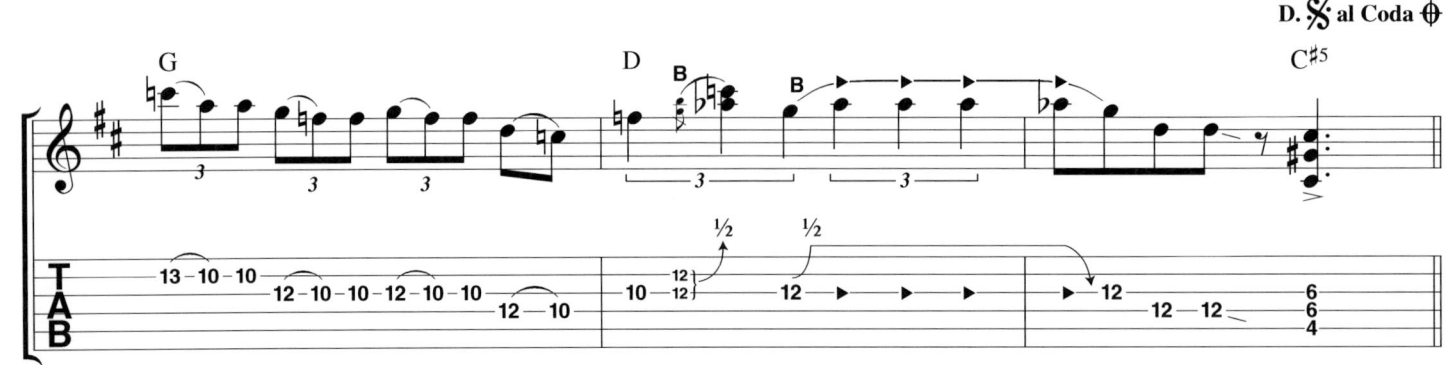

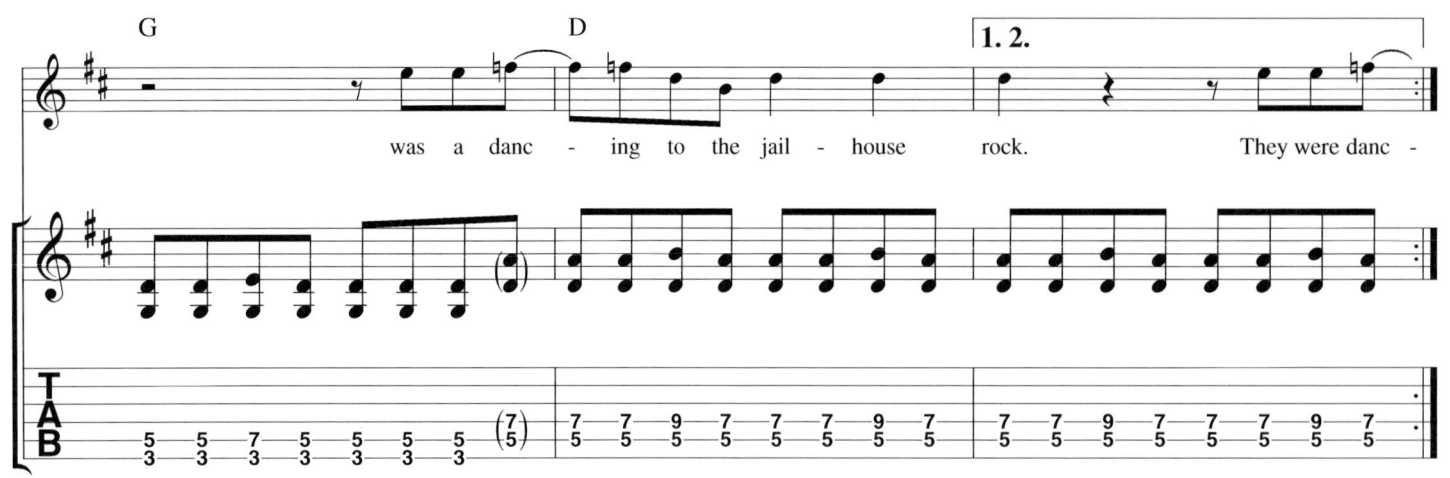
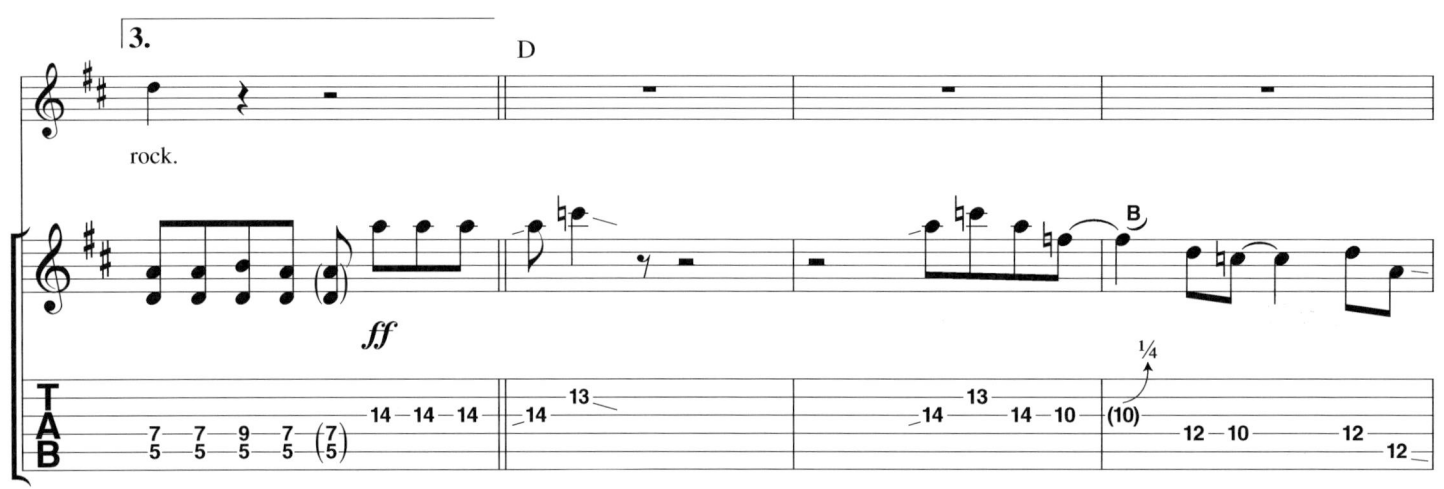
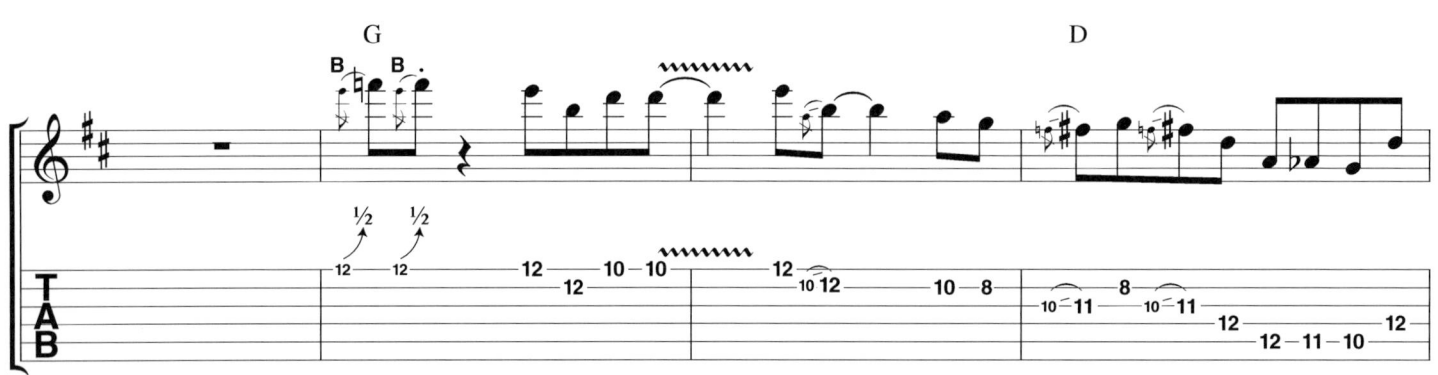
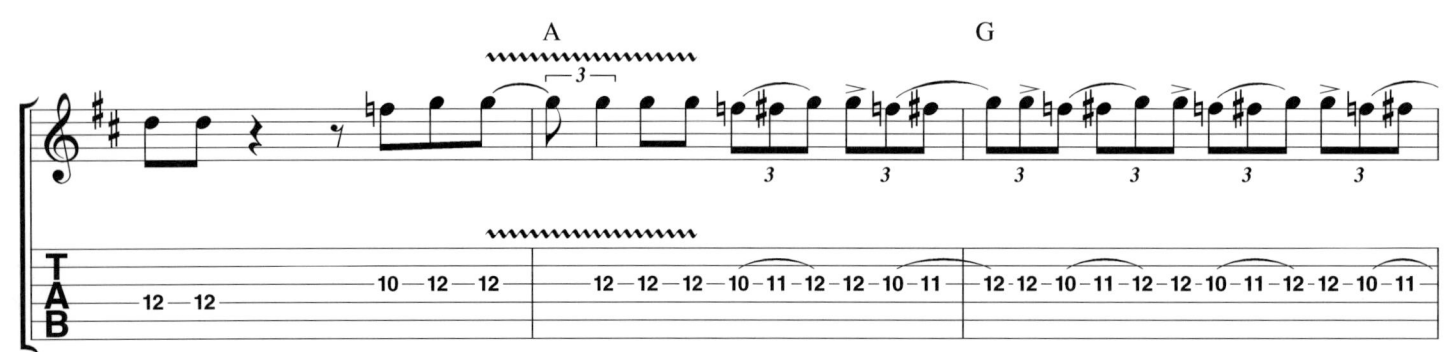

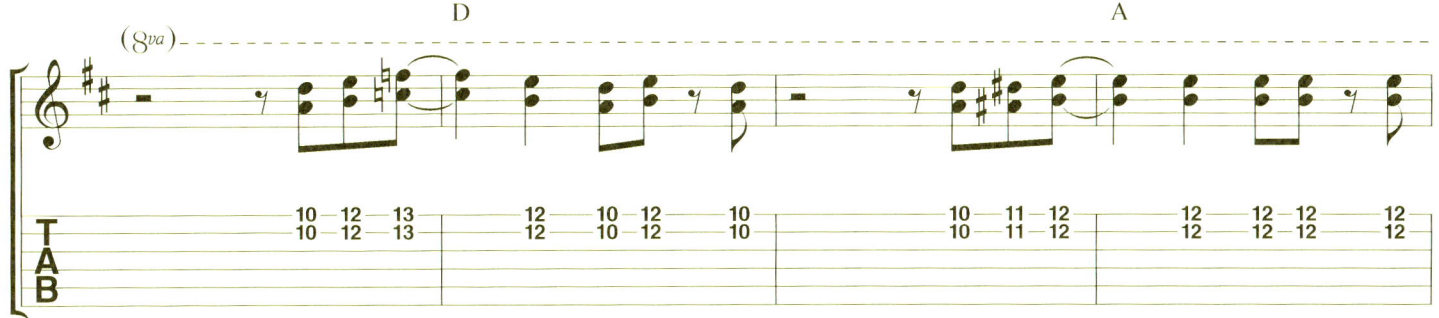

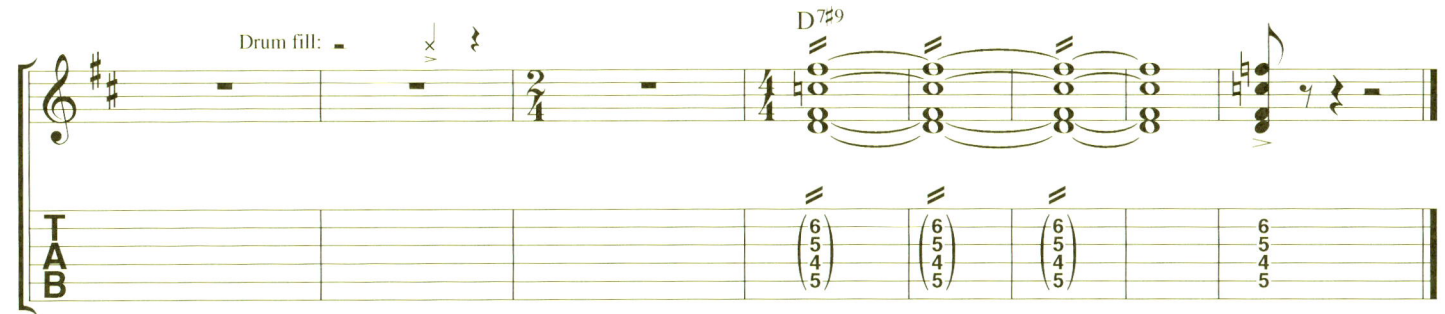

theme from rawhide

Music by Dimitri Tiomkin. Words by Ned Washington

© Copyright 1958 Largo Music Incorporated/Volta Music Corporation/Patti Washington Music, USA.
BMG Music Publishing Limited, Bedford House, 69-79 Fulham High Street, London SW6 3JW.
All Rights Reserved. International Copyright Secured.

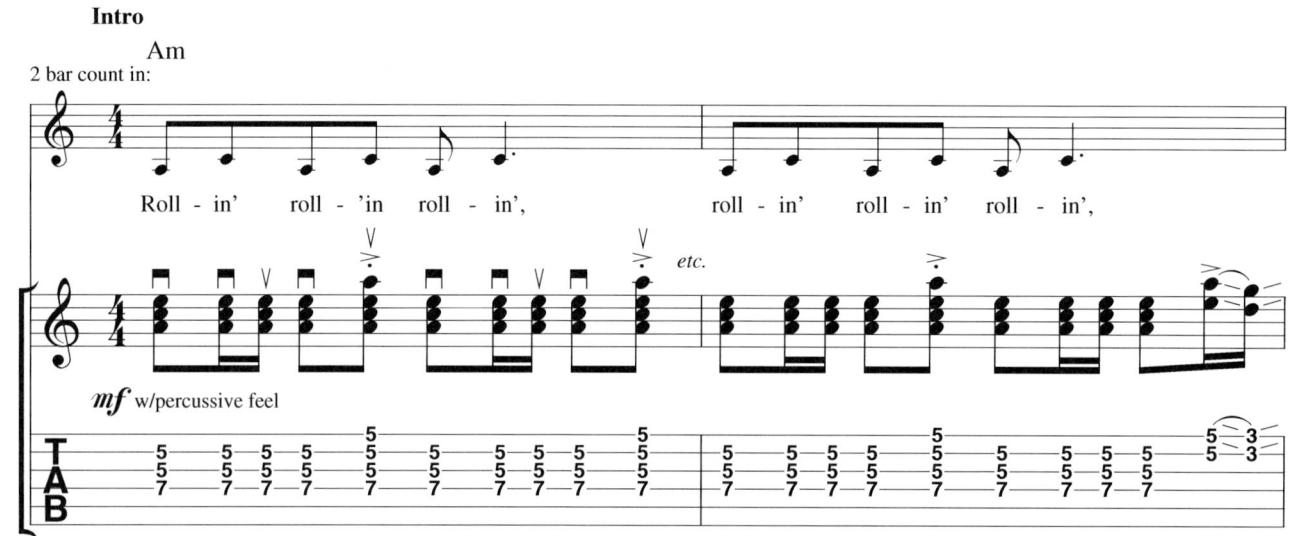

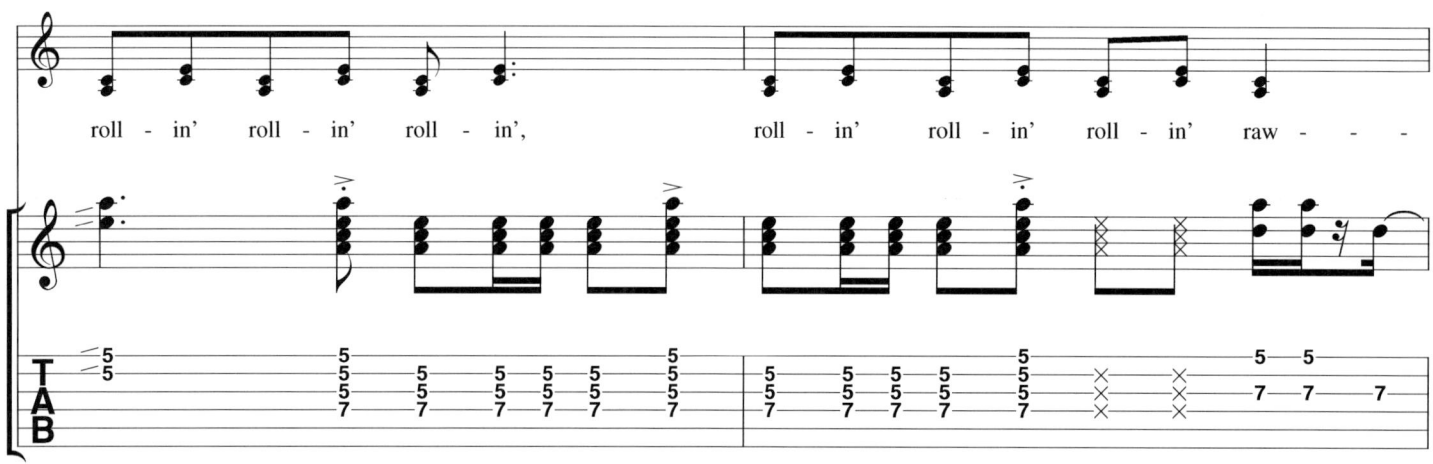

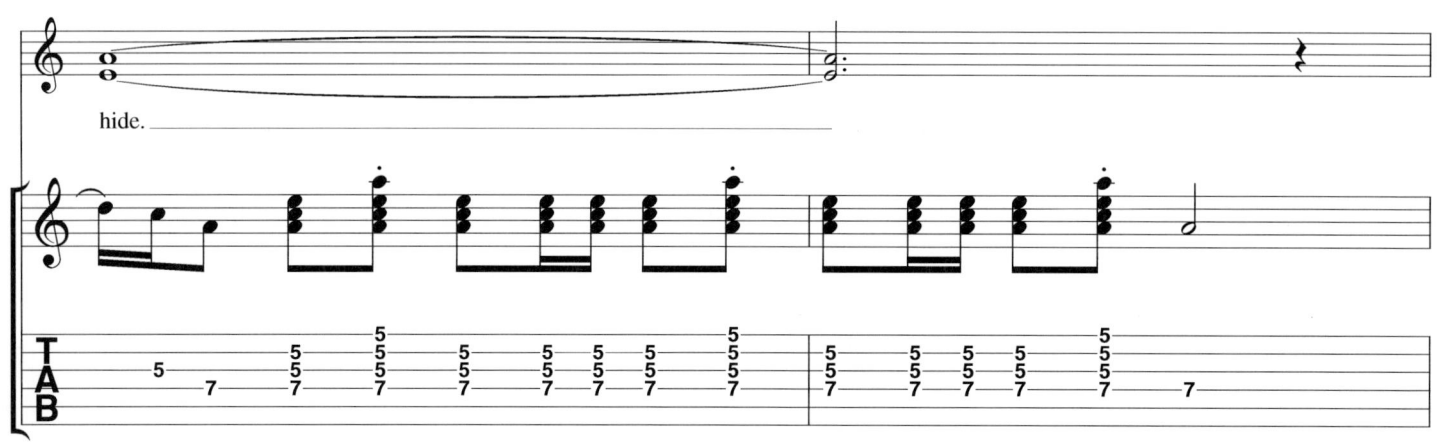

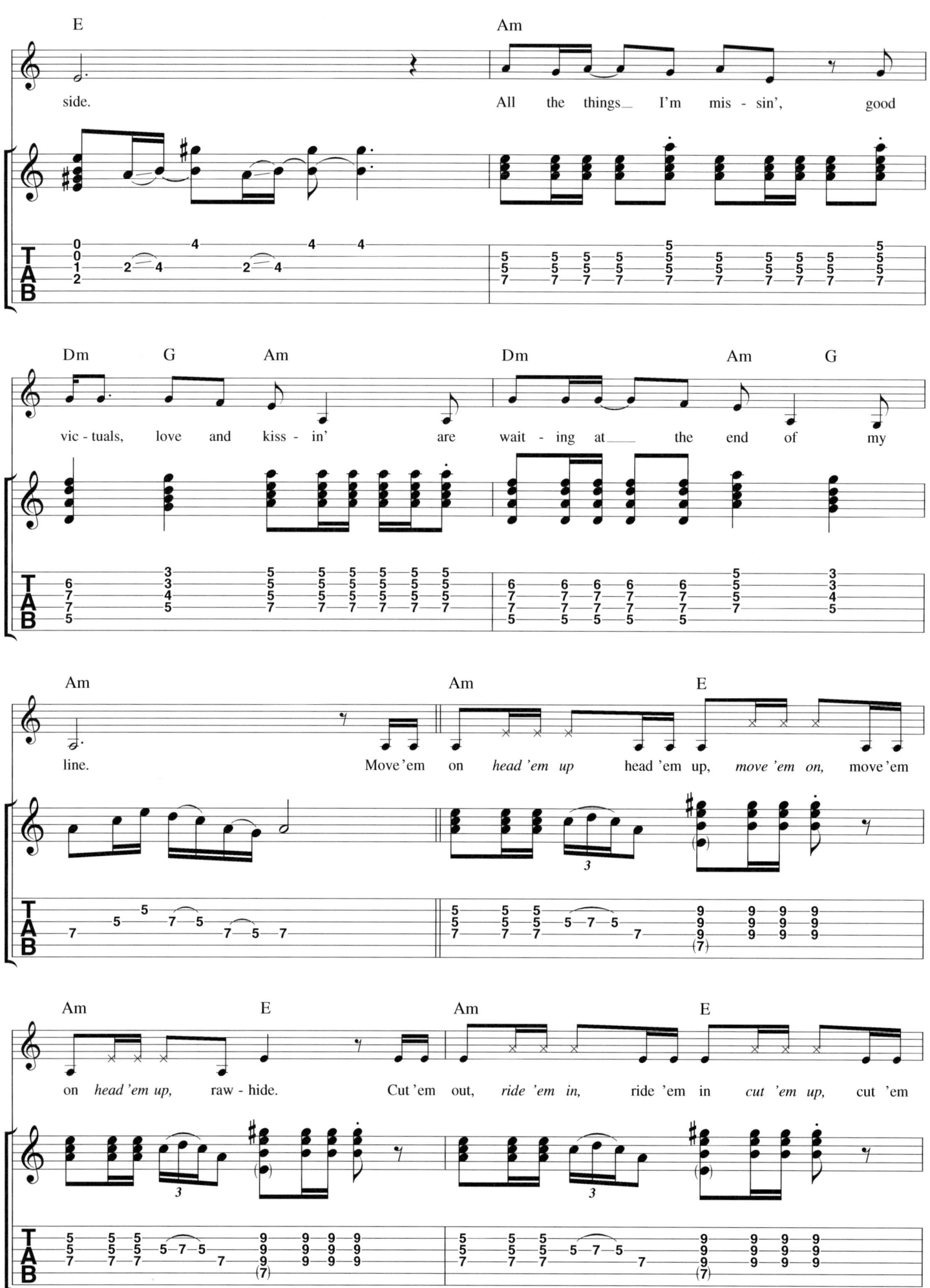

shake a tail feather

Words & Music by Otis Hayes, Andre Williams & Verlie Rice

© Copyright 1967 Vapac Music Incorporated, USA.
Edward Kassner Music Company Limited, Exmouth House, 11 Pine Street, London EC1R 0JH.
All Rights Reserved. International Copyright Secured.

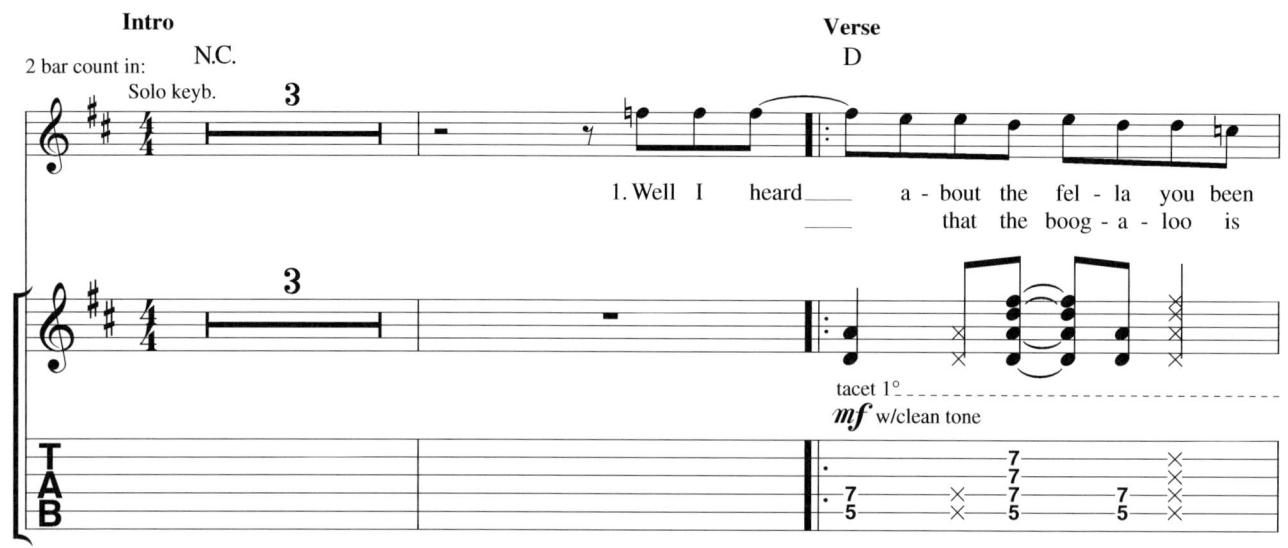

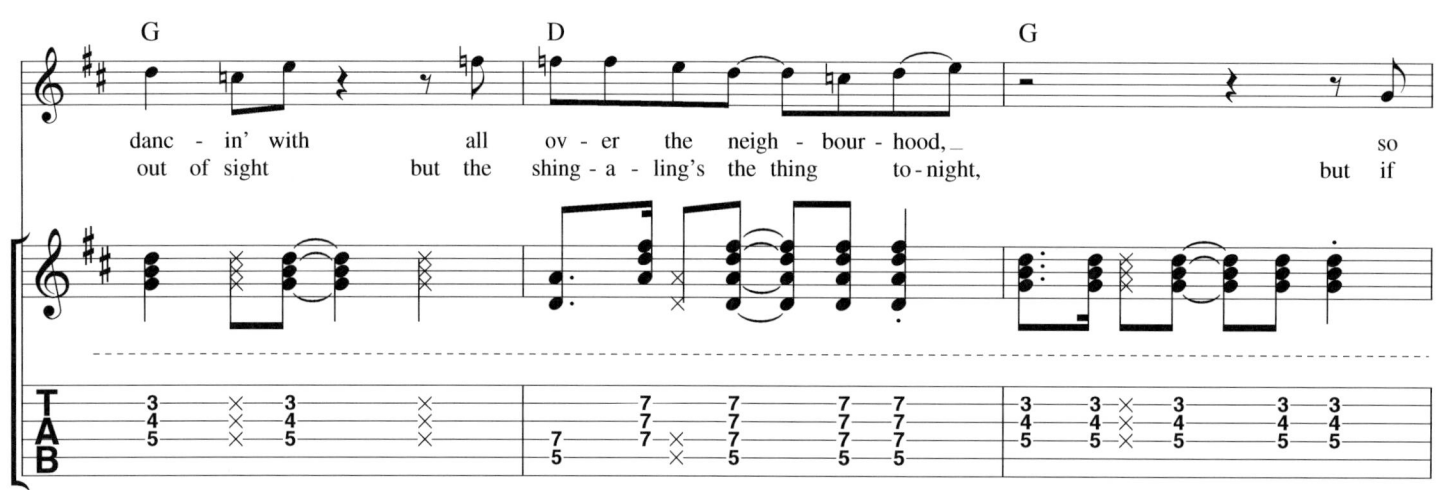

34

sweet home chicago

Words & Music by Robert Johnson

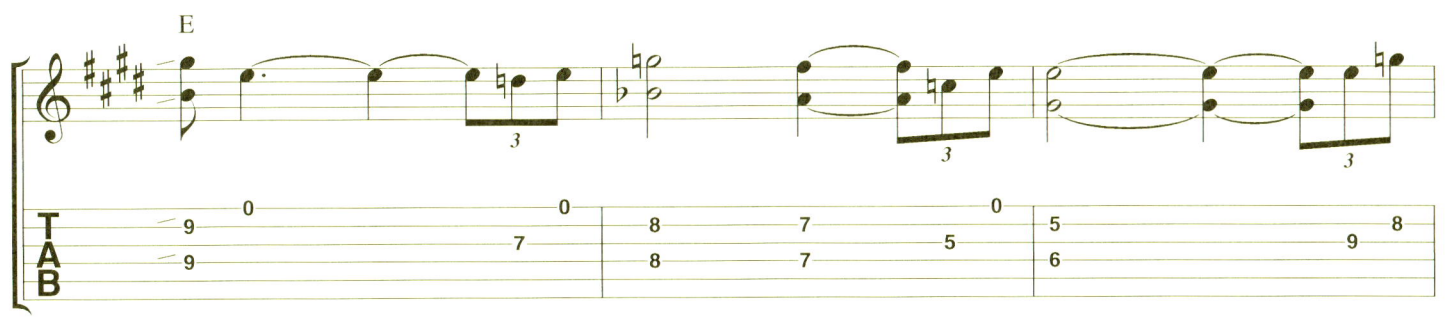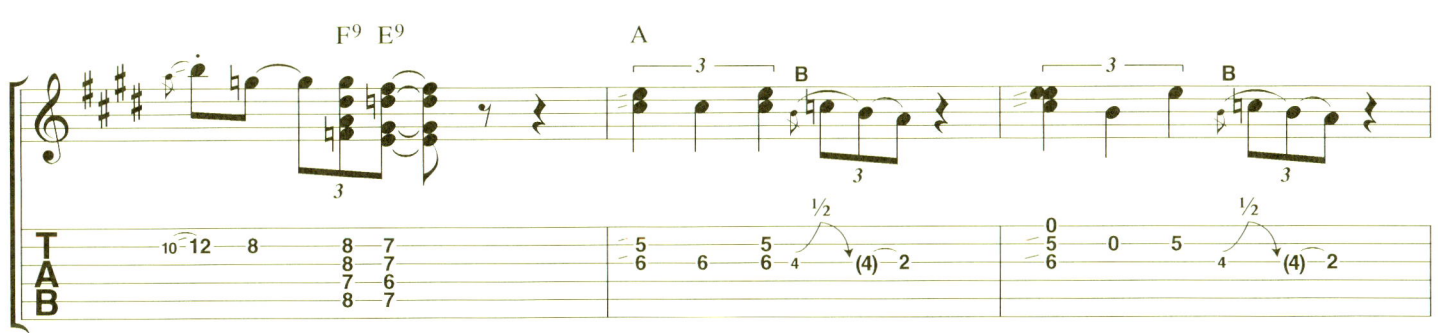

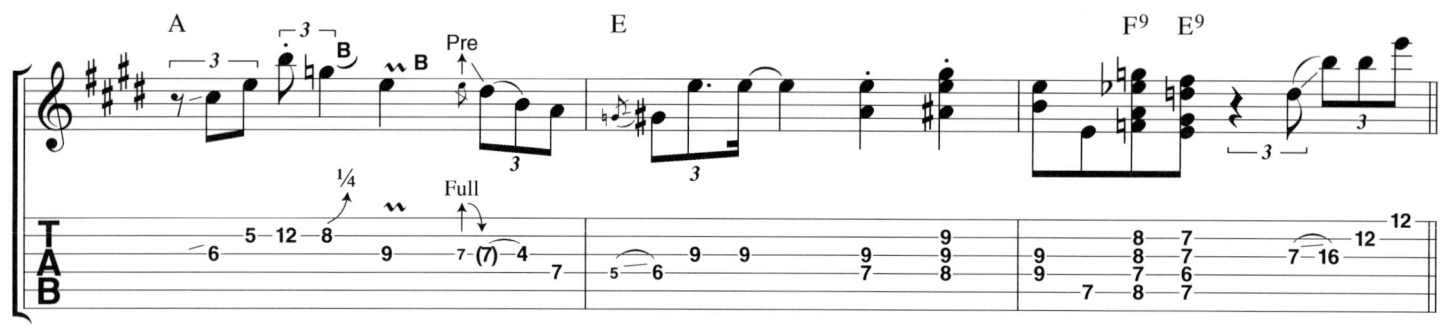
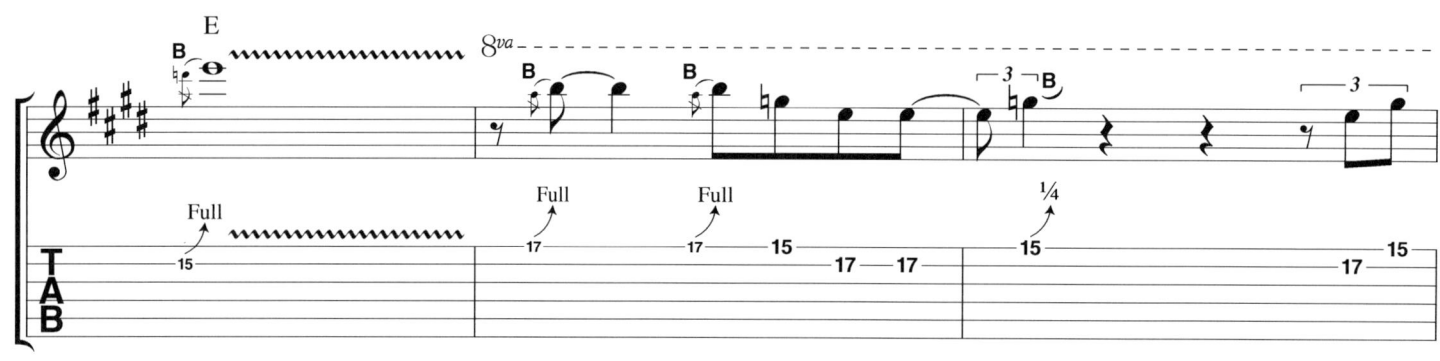
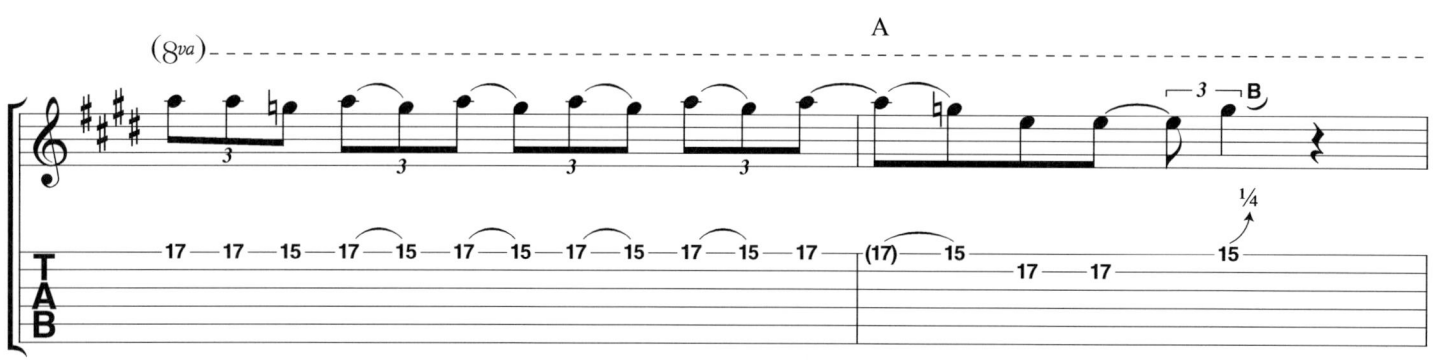
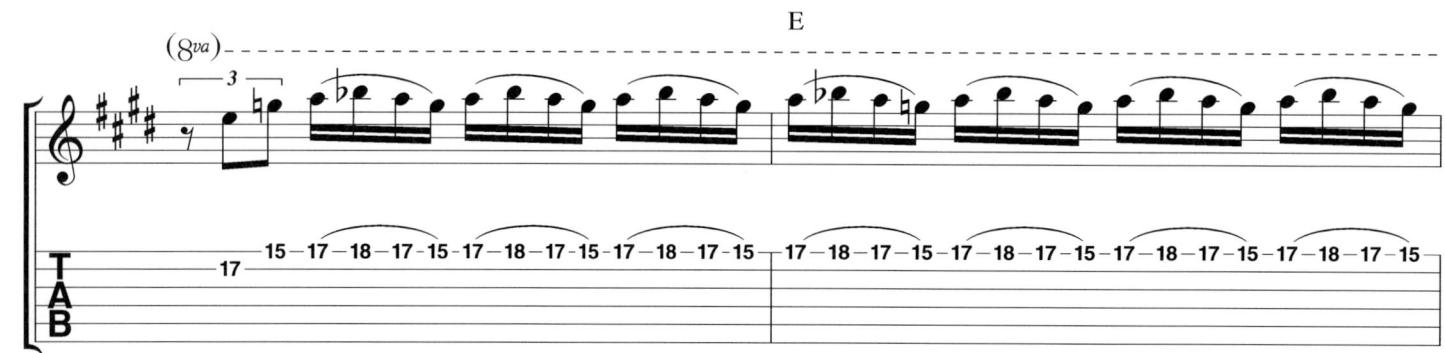

✦ **Coda**

1° & 2° Tenor solo
3° & 4° Piano solo
5° – 8° Brass section

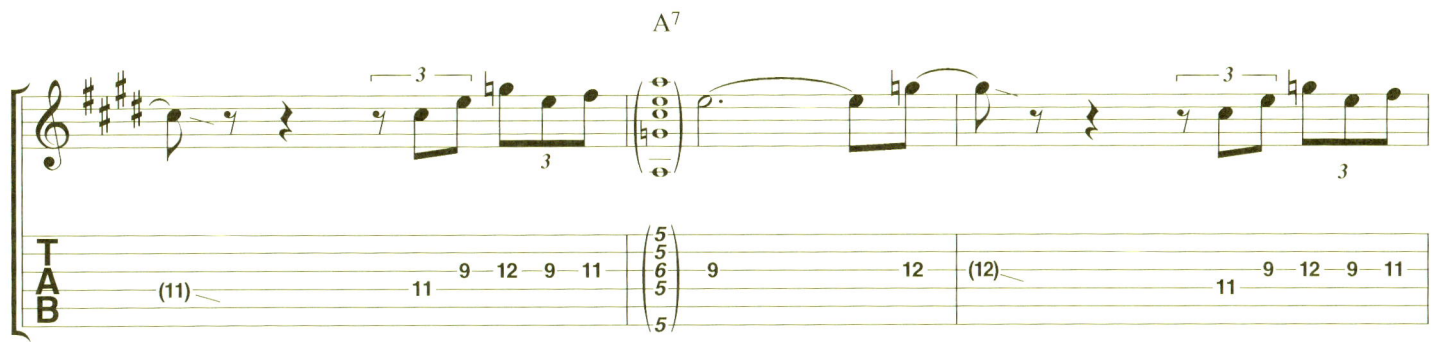

47

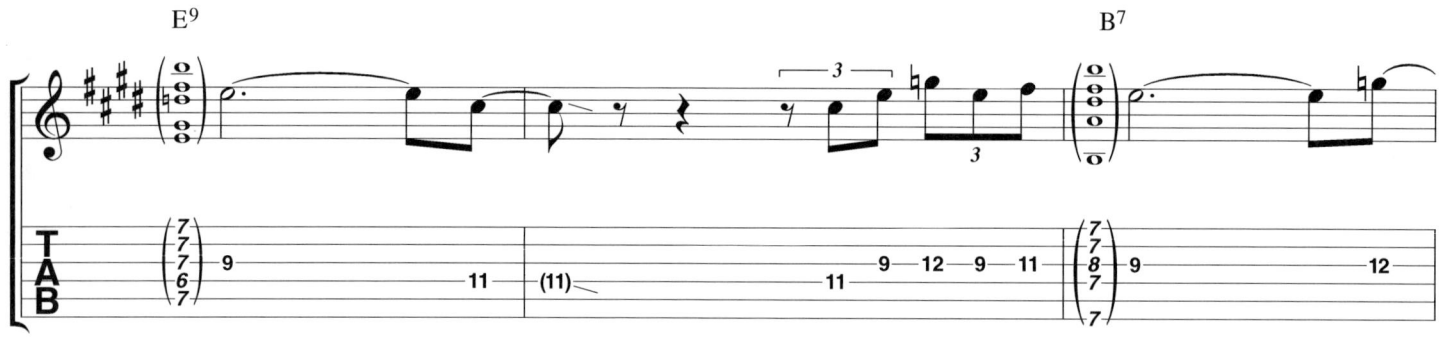
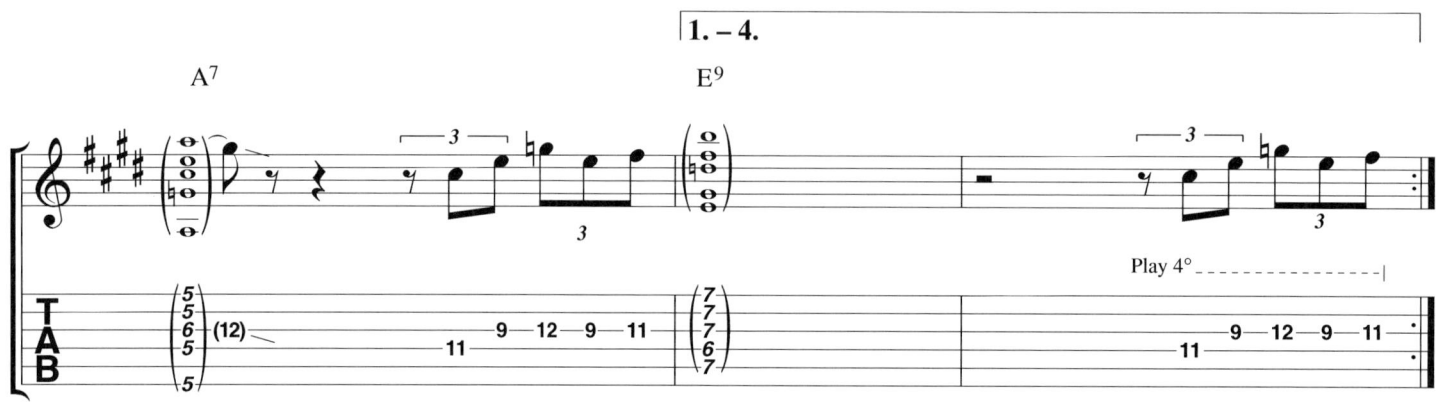

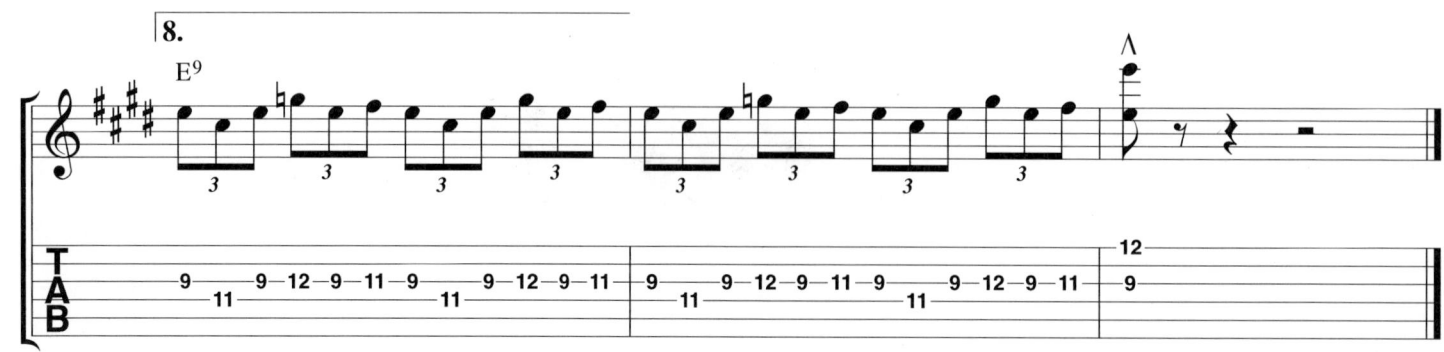

48